THINKING MOVES A-Z

METACOGNITION MADE SIMPLE

by Roger Sutcliffe, Tom Bigglestone & Jason Buckley

To access resources and the latest opportunities with Thinking Moves, go to:

www.dialogueworks.co.uk/thinking-moves

Published by:

The Philosophy Man Ltd
7 Tower Road, Writtle, Chelmsford,
CM1 3NR, UK
Email: office@thephilosophyman.com
Web: www.thephilosophyman.com
Tel: +44 (0) 1245 830123

Dialogue Works Ltd
59 Falkland Road, London,
NW5 2XB, UK
Email: bobhouse@dialogueworks.co.uk
Web: www.dialogueworks.co.uk
Tel: +44 (0) 7763 125 887

All rights reserved. No part of this publication may be reproduced, stored in a retrieval system or transmitted in any form, or by any means, electronic, mechanical, photocopying, recording or otherwise, without the prior permission of the publishers.

© Roger Sutcliffe, Jason Buckley & Tom Bigglestone 2019

ACKNOWLEDGEMENTS

As well as thanking Jason and Tom for the invaluable help they have given me in bringing the A–Z to fruition, I should like to thank Kay Williams and Kerim Hudson for wrangling the book towards its finished form and Sara Liptai for the support, both intellectual and motivational, she gave me at critical times. But no one has enabled me to sustain my focus on this project over the years more than my wife, Vivien, to whom I express the deepest gratitude.

Roger Sutcliffe

CONTENTS

2	Introduction
3	How This Book Is Organised
4	Thinking Moves A-Z List
5	Thinking Moves Coaching Questions
6-57	Thinking Moves
58–59	Thinking Grooves
60–61	Using Thinking Moves in School and Life
62–63	Memorising the Moves
64	Connections with Other Thinking Schemes
65	Training
66	About the Authors
67	Index of Activities

INTRODUCTION

All teaching teaches thinking. Even rote learning teaches remembering as well as individual facts. What we encourage in this book is simply teaching the thinking 'out loud' – drawing attention to the Thinking Moves students already use in school and in everyday life, so that they can become master thinkers, able to choose the right tool for the job in hand. In short, *Thinking Moves A–Z* is a framework for developing metacognition.

We have used the device of an A–Z of 26 Thinking Moves for ease of learning, and because that turns out to be a 'Goldilocks' level of detail – specific enough to be directly useful, general enough to be flexible. So, for example, **Connect** is preferred to the broader 'relationship'; **Infer** is preferred to the more specific 'deduction'.

We have made sure they are all workable "moves", such as thinking **Ahead** or **Back**, rather than longer-term dispositions or character traits, such as resilience or empathy. We wanted to avoid the response, *"That's a good idea. But what does it look like in practice?"* Instead, we wanted the moves to be practical already, so that self-contained examples can be readily found in students' own thinking or expressed in a few sentences.

"Thinking moves. It moves people, communities and societies...forwards, backwards, sideways... even round in circles. This book helps teachers to come to terms with how to move thinking in young people so that it is productive and positive in addressing challenge and opportunity.

The structure of the book and its accessibility mean that the approaches described will allow teachers to fit thinking constructively and coherently into their evolving practice with the result that it becomes natural to think deeply. In this way, thinking moves...it moves awareness, understanding and learning in young people."

Mick Waters, Professor of Education

Today's educators know the importance of metacognition, thinking skills and academic vocabulary. In order for learning to be meaningful, pupils need to acquire and utilise a thinking vocabulary with which to synthesise their knowledge, values and skills. Incorporating the work of Claxton, Costa and Richhart, in Thinking Moves A-Z: Metacognition for Everyday Learning, Sutcliffe and his team have provided us with an essential tool for this. Each Thinking Move is examined and analysed, alongside a set of synonyms and activities in a clear and user-friendly guide, so that any teacher who wishes their students to have meaningful learning experiences can provide them with the help of this excellent toolkit for providing thinking vocabulary and metacognition.

Tracey Smith, Headteacher, New Marston School

HOW THIS BOOK IS ORGANISED

A table on the next page presents the Moves, along with two key synonyms. These synonyms not only clarify the concept behind each Move but can be used routinely instead of the Moves, once the scheme has been memorised (see pp. 64 – 65) and operationalised. In a second table, each Move is linked with a key coaching question, for use in any context. Like the questions used by counsellors, their object is not to give advice, but to draw out from students their own best thinking.

In the heart of the book, each Move is presented into two sections. The orange highlighted area contains an icon for the Move, its key synonyms, a couple more elicitation questions, and an explanation in the sort of language you might use when introducing it to students. The remainder continues with the teacher in mind.

The left column gives a list of connected vocabulary, the first four words of which are other verb synonyms to show the range of the move. The main list is of other associated words that would be part of a good thinker's vocabulary, from the everyday to more academic language. The final words in that list point to the intellectual virtue shown by a person who deliberately practises the move. Someone who regularly thinks back is good at recollection and reflection. This is an important aspect of the scheme, designed to help people cultivate Thinking Moves as habits or 'mindsets'.

On the facing page, we offer ways to explore the move. Some of these activities, in particular the first for each move, can be done in isolation. They often have an element of fun, to open up discussion of a move without the weight of curriculum content. Others deploy a move in the context of a lesson and can be planned or used opportunistically. Applications, in the red box, point to some of the possibilities across the curriculum. In the violet box, quotations provide inspiration or provocation.

Following the explanations of the individual moves are sections on using the moves, especially within Philosophy for Children, and on Thinking Grooves, sequences of moves. We also summarise how the moves connect to other existing schemes, such as Art Costa's Habits of Mind.

We hope you find these useful in your teaching and that they empower the students who learn from you. You may also find the moves, as we have, an aid to planning, creativity and decision-making in professional and wider life. Please do share with us the new applications for the moves that you develop and students' reactions to them.

THINKING MOVES A-Z LIST

	THINKING MOVES	EVERYDAY SYNONYMS	ALTERNATIVE SYNONYMS
A	AHEAD	PREDICT	AIM
B	BACK	REMEMBER	REFLECT
C	CONNECT	LINK	LIKEN
D	DIVIDE	SEPARATE	LIST
E	EXPLAIN	SAY HOW	CLARIFY
F	FORMULATE	SUGGEST	PROPOSE
G	GROUP	SORT	CLASS
H	HEADLINE	SUMMARISE	DISTIL
I	INFER	DEDUCE	TAKE FROM
J	JUSTIFY	GIVE REASON	ARGUE
K	KEYWORD	HIGHLIGHT	PINPOINT
L	LISTEN/LOOK	NOTICE	GATHER
M	MAINTAIN	BELIEVE	AFFIRM
N	NEGATE	DISAGREE	OPPOSE
O	ORDER	SEQUENCE	ARRANGE
P	PICTURE	IMAGINE	PUT YOURSELF
Q	QUESTION	ASK	WONDER
R	RESPOND	ANSWER	REPLY
S	SIZE	ESTIMATE	QUANTIFY
T	TEST	DOUBT	CHECK
U	USE	TRY OUT	APPLY
V	VARY	CHANGE	ALTER
W	WEIGH UP	DECIDE	JUDGE
X	eXEMPLIFY	GIVE EXAMPLE	ILLUSTRATE
Y	YIELD	ACCEPT	CONCEDE
Z	ZOOM	FOCUS ON	SURVEY

THINKING MOVES COACHING QUESTIONS

	THINKING MOVES	COACHING QUESTIONS
A	AHEAD	What do you think will happen?
B	BACK	What were the last two ideas?
C	CONNECT	How do those connect?
D	DIVIDE	How is that different?
E	EXPLAIN	How do you mean?
F	FORMULATE	What ideas have people got?
G	GROUP	How would you sort these into groups?
H	HEADLINE	How would you say that in one sentence?
I	INFER	If that's true, what else is true?
J	JUSTIFY	Can you say why?
K	KEYWORD	Which five words are most important here?
L	LISTEN/LOOK	What do you notice?
M	MAINTAIN	Who is a "yes"?
N	NEGATE	Who is a "no"?
O	ORDER	What's the best way to organise this?
P	PICTURE	What do you see when you picture this?
Q	QUESTION	What's the juiciest question here?
R	RESPOND	What do you say to that?
S	SIZE	What sort of number are we talking?
T	TEST	How could you tell if that's true?
U	USE	How can you use it?
V	VARY	How else could we think?
W	WEIGH UP	Which choice has more back-up?
X	eXEMPLIFY	Can you give me an example?
Y	YIELD	Can you disagree with yourself?
Z	ZOOM	What's the big/little picture?

AHEAD

Predict – Aim

What do you think will happen?
What are you aiming for?

You do this sort of thinking everyday – when you wake up, you're already thinking about what will happen that day. There are lots of ways to think ahead – you might be predicting what will happen next in a story, getting ready for something, setting yourself a challenge, or be looking forward expectantly to a special occasion.

Look forward
Expect
Hope
Target

Future
Goal
End
Means
Ambition
Risk
Precaution
Foresight
Probable
Possible
Inevitable
Consequence

Anticipation
Resolution

Predicting, preparing, intending and hoping are all ways of bringing the future into the present. Anticipating what will, or might, happen enables us to be ready when it does. Foretelling dangers enables us to minimise harm, whilst foreseeing opportunities enables us to maximise benefits.

In school, thinking ahead is crucial for forming aims and targets, setting short-term goals for group work and preparing revision timetables. (*"How should I organise these notes so they will help me revise?"*)

With young students, we do most of the thinking ahead for them, but getting them to think ahead for themselves is important for developing independence. (*"What's needed in today's schoolbag?"*)

What Would Happen Then?

This storytelling game thinks ahead through chains of predictions. Start with an imaginative scenario, e.g. *"What would happen if you were invisible?"* Take the first suggestion offered, e.g. *"You'd be lonely because nobody could see you."* Then ask, *"What would happen then, because of that?"* Continue the chain, recapping occasionally or breaking into pairs to generate new ideas. "Because of that" is the key element, as events in stories are not random, they follow in a chain of consequences.

Won't, Could, Will

Get some predictions for what won't happen next (this helps to narrow the domain of reasonable answers) and what could happen next. Then, from the candidate 'coulds', (four or five are enough), see if the students can agree, with reasons, an **Order** of likelihood. (Can they be certain of any event?)

Project Projections

Projecting one's thinking into the future is essential for a successful project. Next time there's a group task that lasts two lessons or more, pause the students after the first lesson and ask them, *"If you carry on like this, will you achieve what you want to achieve?"* They can reflect on current progress and predict how they will fare against their deadline. They might need to change tack!

"If you can look into the seeds of time, and say which grain will grow and which will not, speak then unto me."
Banquo in William Shakespeare's *Macbeth*

"Begin with an end in mind."
Stephen Covey

Applications: What won't / could / will happen...?

Music
...later in a composition

ICT
...in a robot's response to an algorithm

RS
...in a Hindu wedding

BACK

Remember – Reflect

What can you recall from …?
Let's take some time to review/reflect!

You do a lot of this – especially after something enjoyable or exciting, like remembering a day out or a successful game. Of course, sometimes you may remember things that didn't go so well. This isn't necessarily a bad thing though – because it could help you to make things better in the future.

Recall
Rehearse
Think again
Chew over

Beginning
Origin
Past
History
Ancestry
Forerunner
Memory
Recollection
Reminiscent
Replay
Second thoughts
Turning point

Recollection
Reflection

At its simplest, learning is organising new information and ideas into our existing way of thinking. A lot of this process takes place unconsciously, but deliberate, regular reflection is the high road to good learning. If one move 'rules all', it is this, metacognitive, one. It demands that you stop thinking (ironically!) and think again about the moves you have made in the past and could make in the future, not least the final move in the A–Z: **Zoom**. You might decide to zoom out to see the big, general picture, or to zoom in on something in particular.

There are other ways of organising and memorising ideas. Converting information into stories or sequences (such as acrostics or an A–Z) can help, as can creating **Pictures** in your mind. Psychologists recommend thinking back often on what you are trying to learn, as well as trying to **Headline** or summarise it. They also say that sleeping well helps.

Thinking back can also be a way of dealing with present or future challenges. This is particularly important for nurturing resilience in the face of difficulty: once a challenge has been overcome, recalling how intimidating it seemed at the start can reduce the trepidation next time.

Remains of the Day

This is a memory game, but it also shows how accounts of the past are always selective and usually subjective. In a quick, individual exercise, each student writes down 10 things they remember happening during the previous school day that don't happen every week (so as to avoid just a list of times of the day). You can then compare the lists and notice the things that some remember but others do not.

Remains of the Lesson

Half way through a lesson or at the end, invite students to recall steps in the lesson so far. The steps can be simple events: *"How did the lesson start?" "What did I ask you to do then?" "What happened next?"* For more challenge, you can ask what people said, or just for 'ideas'. You or the students might represent the steps in a flow chart, as a record of the lesson.

Pause for Reflection / Reflective Journals

The importance of pausing occasionally during a lesson for a minute's private reflection is underestimated. Encourage students to have a reflective journal, in which they record not only the main ideas just introduced or discussed (see **Keyword** later), but also random reflections of their own about their experiences or understandings.

"Life must be lived forwards, but can only be understood backwards."
Soren Kierkegaard

"Without reflection, we go blindly on our way, creating more unintended consequences."
Margaret J Wheatley

Applications:
What happened...

Drama
...in the previous scene?

PE
...the last time your team had a free-kick?

History
...when we last learnt about Edward I?

CONNECT

Link – Liken

How are X and Y related?
How are X and Y similar?

Your brain has been making connections pretty much since you were born – linking one thing with another. Maybe you find them in the same place, or they happen at the same time, or they might be alike in some way. You can also link words or ideas together – such as the idea of 'bear', with the idea of 'grisly' – or with the almost opposite idea of 'cuddly'. Creative thinking often involves linking ideas that no one has put together before, such as 'Paddington' and 'bear'.

Put together
Associate
Match
Compare

Similar
Alike
Resemblance
Identical
Relationship
Common
Comparison
Comparatively
Correlation
Relevant
Analogy
Metaphor

Association
Assimilation

The human brain seems primed to make an almost infinite number of connections, connecting one idea with another by spotting some relationship or similarity between them – even when presented with random pairs of words such as 'melon' and 'hedgehog'.

Connecting ideas systematically is what makes for deep learning and understanding, rather than surface knowledge and rote definitions. For example, making connections helps learners understand the whole water cycle, rather than just the isolated definitions of the stages, because it is the inter-relationships between stages that are significant.

Extensive research suggests that such understanding can't happen from chalk and talk: learners must actively make the connections.

Alike Like This

Get an idea for an object from a volunteer, e.g. a mug. Someone thinks of something that is like a mug in some way, such as, *"A mug and a glass are alike like this – you can drink from both of them."* The chain continues with a suggestion for something that is like a glass in a different way, for example, *"A glass and window are alike like this – they're both breakable"*, then *"A window and a hole in a wall are alike like this – you can see through them"*, *"A hole in a wall and an injury are alike like this – they can both be caused by a bomb"*, and so on.

Missing Connections

Make two lists in columns of random nouns (concrete or abstract), perhaps suggested by students. List A should have 5–10 items, and List B 6–11, i.e. one extra. In pairs, students should copy the lists and connect (literally with a line) each item in A with one item in B, making sure they can explain the connections. Initially, pairs can share their results with each other informally. When all pairs are ready, see which item in B is hardest to connect with and perhaps why.

Joined-up Thinking (Last Three to Speak)

This is a bit like *Remains of the Lesson* (see **Back**) but with a focus on connecting ideas. After any sequence of three (significant) contributions by students, call for a pause and ask, *"Who were the last three to speak?"* Give students a little time to recollect, then put them in pairs to agree answers to *"What did each person say?"* and *"How did what they say connect?"* Repeated practice of this exercise will pay dividends in better dialogue – more attentive listening and more constructive speaking.

"Creativity is just connecting things."
Steve Jobs

"Shall I compare thee to a summer's day?"
William Shakespeare

Applications:
How does…

Art
…Impressionism relate to Expressionism?

Philosophy
…that question link to this one?

Maths
…this sum help us solve that equation?

DIVIDE

Separate – List

How are X and Y different?
Let's list the differences!

Before your brain can even make connections between things, it has to recognise that some things are different from others. It has to separate them out or differentiate them. Otherwise you would not be able to spot danger, for example, or find your food. And you would not hear different words, let alone understand them.

Tell apart
Distinguish
Take apart
Analyse

Different
Opposite
Distinction
Exception
Contrast
Whereas
Part
Element
Feature
Complex
Binary
Borderline

Differentiation
Dissection

'Telling the difference' is one of the first things learners are asked to practise. Learning language itself involves a huge amount of differentiation of sounds, words and meanings. Speakers of one language can find it hard to notice that two sounds from another language are different. Students need to be trained in spotting all sorts of differences – between experiences, objects, situations, words, ideas – so that they can respond appropriately.

Careful analysis becomes more important as a learner progresses through the education system. In Science you learn to dissect things into parts or elements. In History little details matter, and in Art you become aware of finer features and aspects of sensory experience.

Same but Different

Point out that everyone can divide the room into many different objects. (You could ask, how many?) This is a basic ability. Then say that it is more challenging to recognise differences between two objects that are the same (that is, are given the same name, e.g. book, pen, table, window, etc.) Pairs are invited to choose any such objects and list as many differences as they can. To end, invite each pair to say what is the biggest difference between their chosen objects.

Two but One (Odd One Out)

For this you'll need sets of three objects, pictures or words in which there are similarities between each pair that differentiate them from the other two. The game is to make claims about the odd one out, using the formula, *"Two... but one..."*.

For example, with a plane, an eagle and a horse: *"Two are means of transport but one isn't"*, *"Two are natural but one is man-made"*, *"Two can fly but one has to walk."*

Sim/Diff chart

This is a 'compare and contrast' exercise, useful in any subject. Two items (objects, characters, events) to be compared will head columns 1 and 3. The middle column is headed 'in common', and features or aspects the items have in common are listed here. Features that are different, i.e. unique, for each of the items are listed in the appropriate column. The exercise is best done firstly in pairs, then 'twos into fours' – with each pair adding features from the other's lists. This chart is a simpler version of Hyerle's Double Bubble Map.

"Every thing is what it is, and not another thing."
Joseph Butler

"Fools ignore complexity. Geniuses remove it."
Alan Perlis

Applications:
What are the differences between...

Design
...cantilever and suspension bridges?

PSHE
...two branches of government?

English
...these two war poems?

EXPLAIN

Say how – Clarify

How do we explain this?
Could you clarify what you mean?

If you don't understand what is going on, or how things work, you might ask someone to explain – to tell you, as in a story, what causes what, or how things or people relate to each other. A good explanation makes something complicated easier to understand.

Relate
Account for
Make clear
Define

Because
Story
Narrative
Cause
Effect
Behaviour
Motive
Law
Account
(Make) Sense
Process
Factor

Narration
Definition

Explanations assist our understanding of the world – how it is put together and how it works. The ability to explain well represents a fundamental difference between learning a term's 'surface' meaning and 'deep' learning, i.e. 'deeply felt' meaning. It is the ability to use a term in several contexts and to break it down for others, perhaps employing analogies or metaphors.

We commonly explain by outlining a sequence of events, saying how or why they have happened, giving a context and causes. But we can equally well explain how parts fit together in a whole, as when an architect explains how their building holds together.

If something is badly explained, there can be a call for it to be explained again – that is, for the meaning of the original explanation to be clarified. This may sometimes require a precise definition of just one word. Note that 'explaining' (saying how or why something has happened) is different from 'justifying' (saying why you have done something).

Why Chain

This game involves explaining the causal chains behind events and situations. Start with a problem, large or small, real or imaginary. The student who proffers the problem is the first link in the chain. The next student gives a reason why that happens, the next a reason why **that** happens and so on.

A: There are tons of plastic waste in the sea." Why?
B: Because people use bottles once and throw them away." Why?
C: Because they don't cost much." Why?
D: Because they are cheap to make." Why?

If you make the thinking physical, by getting people to stand next to one another as the chain builds, you can turn your chain into a 'Why Tree' with different branches and rival explanations of reasons previously given.

What were the Dominoes?

This can be used to encourage students to explain the sequence of causes of any event, occurrence or phenomenon, in any subject. Draw a row of dominoes on the board, and write the event/occurrence/phenomenon on the furthest right. Get students working in pairs to label the remaining dominoes. Each domino has to be the cause of the one to its right, and so you end up with a set of chain-reacting factors, each causing the next.

"The way historians explain things is by telling a story."
Donal Kagan

"Whatever cannot be said clearly is probably not being thought clearly either."
Peter Singer

Applications:
Can you make a 'Why Chain' for...

PE
...over-stretching causing injury

Science
...a heatwave occurring

English
...the character Bottom ending up with the head of a donkey

FORMULATE

Suggest – Propose

Does anyone have a suggestion?
Can you find a way of expressing your idea?

When babies cry or smile, it is obvious they have feelings. At some point, they must have ideas, too, but they cannot formulate, or give form to, those ideas until they have the words to do so – beginning, probably, with 'Mama' or 'Dadda'. After that, they can gradually grow in their ability to express their feelings and to come up with ideas, even theories, of their own.

Come up with
Express
Invent
Speculate

Idea
Draft
Concept
Brainwave
Maybe
Guess
Intuition
Proposal
Improvisation
Solution
Theory
Hypothesis

Conceptualisation

Jason Buckley often uses riddles as an icebreaker in workshops. With one class, he was rather baffled by the stony silence. He asked why, unusually, nobody was guessing. A student replied, *"Because we don't know the answer."* But that, of course, is exactly when a guess is needed!

Nurturing a classroom culture that celebrates the expression of ideas, from guesses to theories, suggestions to proposals, encourages learners to 'put something out there' and to welcome comment on it. The sooner students realise that you can often build as much on 'wrong' answers as on 'right' ones, the more they will take risks in response to questions, and the more resilient they will become.

The same culture of risk-taking will help students express their feelings more, and more honestly, in response to you or others, and become more confident in formulating opinions in important matters of judgement.

Suggest a Title
Display four pictures or photos that could be interpreted in different ways, then invite students to come up privately with titles for them and write them down. Put them in pairs to talk about their suggestions, and then 'twos into fours' to agree on one title for each picture. (If they can't easily agree, each person can choose one title for one picture.) Compare and discuss the suggested titles, emphasising that each one has its merits, and that you want to celebrate creativity, not cultivate competition.

Ideas for Improvement
Give students time, perhaps between classes, to come up with ideas for improving school life or life at large. Then give them 10 minutes in trios to share their ideas and agree on one that they would like to celebrate.

Pair, Pool, Pick, Pitch
This move is useful for any time you ask for suggestions (e.g. to solve a problem). In pairs, students come up with a suggestion (Pair), before forming a four and sharing with others (Pool). The students then decide which of the two is the better suggestion (Pick) before presenting it to the class (Pitch).

> "Be less curious about people and more curious about ideas."
> Marie Curie

Applications:
Suggest...

Geography
...improvements for a cleaner world

Design
...possible or desirable inventions, e.g. a desk that suits everyone

English
...a poem to express your current feeling or mood

Social Science
...ways to reduce the nation's sugar consumption

Art
...make a doodle or find an interesting picture, then give it a title

GROUP

Sort – Class

Can we sort these into groups?
How could you class or describe this?

You are often sorting things (objects, people, places) into different groups or kinds. For example, when you tidy things away, you put the same things together. Sometimes the group that a particular thing belongs to is obvious. Other times, it might take some careful thought. Palaeontologists have spent years trying to work out which fossils belong to which group or class of dinosaurs.

Assemble
Categorise
Label
Describe

Same
Sort
Kind
Set
Class
Member
Belong
Type
Species
Category
Feature
Characteristic

Organisation
Precision

The ability to group things together in our minds is fundamental to human thought, perhaps even instinctive. We recognise something to be a snake, for example, even though we have never met **this** snake. It is how we make sense of the world and of all the things in it – recognising that some things have so much in common that they can be regarded as the same sort of thing.

Things can belong to lots of different groups at once. A frying pan can be a container, a potential weapon, an essential purchase for a university student. It can also have a 'descriptive' label, such as (something) 'metal/round/shiny/used for cooking.' To describe a particular thing is actually to assign it to a group or class of like things. Encouraging learners to class or describe things in different ways challenges them intellectually and makes them think in original, creative ways.

Sort It Out!

Take two skipping ropes or hoops and create a Venn diagram on the floor so that you can easily demonstrate the idea of 'examples of x go here', 'examples of y go there', and 'examples of both go in the middle'. Label the two rings, for example, 'land creatures / sea creatures', and give each student an example to sort into the correct space, such as a card with an animal or fish on it. You can increase the difficulty by moving from the factual to the contestable. For example, ask students to sort animals into good pets and bad pets. Then suggest that they sort them into those that are OK to eat and those that are not.

Blockbusters

You'll need to google *Blockbusters PPT* to bring this '80s game show into your classroom. Two teams compete to complete a path across the screen, which is a tessellation of hexagons labelled with letters. A team selects a hexagon and has to answer a question of the form, *"What P is an alkali metal that reacts with water, burning with a lilac flame?"* You can get one class to set a grid of questions for another (excellent for revision). Emphasise that each letter labels a group/kind/set/class.

Sorting Hat

This activity can easily be done with any big set or collection of things (objects, events, artworks, chapters, consequences, symbols – anything you can collect and display). Ask students to sort these things into different groups, like the Sorting Hat sorts pupils into houses at Hogwarts. They may spot categories that wouldn't occur to us. When they've finished, they can inspect other groups' efforts and deduce the categorisation chosen.

"Science is the systematic classification of experience."
George Henry Lewe

"If names be not correct, language is not in accordance with the truth of things."
Confucius

Applications:
Sort it out!

Music
...a range of instruments

Science
...a list of elements

History
...causes of an event

HEADLINE

Summarise – Distil

How could we headline what X just said?
Let's summarise/recap the main points...

If you just looked at the headlines of a newspaper, without reading any of the articles, you would still have a pretty good idea of the most important events of the day. Headlines grab attention, are easy to remember and save time. Being able to use a few words to get across the gist of something is helpful in class and in everyday life.

Recap
Abridge
Condense
Outline

Heading
Point
Summary
Abstract
Digest
Gist
In a nutshell
Concise
Précis
Bullet points
Synopsise
Essence
Succinct

Concision

The essence of all forms of summary is the process of boiling down or distilling something into a more condensed form. Sometimes it can help to **Keyword** the main ideas, but a headline will typically be a phrase or sentence rather than individual words.

A successful summariser can process, understand and capture large amounts of information so as to pass on the gist to someone else. It can be very satisfying to come up with a good headline or express an idea with concision.

Summarising is also the bedrock of **Responding** or feeding back. A genuine response requires, firstly, an understanding of what has been said. Summarising is invaluable at every stage of life – from passing on messages to contributing to a boardroom discussion.

Seven-word Summaries

Individually or in pairs, summarise a famous story (book or film) in exactly seven words so others can guess the title. For example, *Boy with multi-coloured coat dreams himself rich.*

Head2Headlines

(Shamelessly adapted from Chris Evans' old breakfast radio show.) A good headline perfectly summarises in a catchy expression. Once you have covered any material, each student devises a headline for this knowledge. For example, on Photosynthesis: PLANT POWER TURNS LIGHT INTO LIVELINESS! or on Right Angles: TO GET THE RIGHT ANGLE, DON'T CUT CORNERS! Students get into threes and each individual creates a headline. Two announce their headline, with the third student judging which one best sums up the material. The judge's headline is then pitted against the winner's, with the loser deciding between them. Last headline standing wins! Winning headlines from all the trios could then be judged by the teacher or by majority vote.

Hold the Front Page!

(A more formal variation of the above.)
When a teacher gives learners a title or learning objective to write at the start of a piece of work, it is the teacher's title for something that doesn't yet belong to the learners. Either instead of or as well as a title, at the end of the work get the learners to write their own, memorable headline in a large font that captures the most important message from what has been learned.

"Much wisdom often goes with brevity of speech."
Sophocles

"If it is possible to cut a word out, always cut it out."
George Orwell

Applications:
Hold the Front Page!
Write a headline that captures...

Politics
...the Prime Minister's speech to Parliament

Art
...this biography of Van Gogh

Geography
...this description of Brazil

INFER

Deduce – Take from

Does anyone have a suggestion?
What might we take from the evidence so far?

To infer is to draw a conclusion, usually from some evidence or from a line of reasoning, a bit like a detective. In class, you might be asked what you can tell from a book or video, but you probably draw lots of conclusions in real life, too, without quite realising it. If you see frost, for example, you might infer that it is cold and decide to dress warmly, without actually putting your thoughts into words.

Figure out
Conclude
Interpret
Generalise

So
Therefore
If ... then
Follow(s)
Logic(al)
Premise
Assumption
Conclusion
Implication
Conjecture
(Not) necessarily
Consistent

Deduction
Induction

Inference takes the form, *"If A (is true), then B (is true)"*, where A is called the 'premise' and B is the 'conclusion'. If B follows **necessarily** from A – typically because of the way A is defined – the reasoning is known as 'formal' or 'deductive' logic, and the conclusion is said to be 'logical' or 'valid'. A conclusion is said to be not logical, or 'illogical', if it does not follow at all from the premise.

Not all arguments have to be **strictly** logical. For example, if you see someone with a runny nose, it would be reasonable enough to infer that they have a cold. But they **might** be suffering from an allergy, not a cold. The conclusion, then, is not a necessary one: it is **probable** rather than certain. This sort of reasoning is called 'informal' or 'inductive', and the conclusion is strictly said to be 'induction' rather than deduction. Inductive reasoning tends to get better with experience, as we learn what is probable/improbable/impossible; deductive reasoning tends to improve as we learn to distinguish between the meanings of words.

Detectives

Students wander around a space until you call for them to pair off. Then, in pairs, they look around the room for something to make a statement about, e.g. *"One of the lights is not working."* One of the pair makes their statement, and the other is given the chance to tell or take something from either the **words** of the statement or the **situation** it describes, e.g. *"There may be something wrong with the light bulb (or the electric supply)."* (The range could be from logically necessary to likely to possible.) On return to their seats, there should be an invitation to celebrate any impressive 'detective work', especially inferences of a necessary or probable nature. The exercise can also be done with students sat in pairs, looking at a photo of an interesting painting (such as *An Experiment on a Bird in the Air Pump*).

Solid, Shaky, Shouldn't

Given a piece of evidence and an inference from it, students indicate with hand signals if they think the conclusion is solid (hand held flat), shaky (hand wobbling) or that the inference doesn't follow (thumbs down), e.g. *"This floats, so it can't be made of metal."* Students could be encouraged to assist with the creation of a range of inferences, writing down one that is certain, one that is probable, and one that is only just possible.

What Follows?

Take any central statement or scenario to do with the lesson of the day or week. The task is to come up with as many logical inferences as possible from the statement. For example: *Martin Luther King was a civil rights leader who marched to Selma.* What else must be true? (e.g. He visited Alabama; he was not alone; the march had a point...)

"From a drop of water a logician could infer the possibility of an Atlantic or a Niagara without having seen or heard of one or the other."
Sherlock Holmes in A. C. Doyle's *A Study in Scarlet*

"We are here and it is now. The way I see it is, after that, everything tends towards guesswork.... I could be wrong. Not being certain is what being a philosopher is all about."
Didactylos in Terry Pratchett's *Small Gods*

Applications:
What follows?

English
...that Scrooge wanted Cratchit to work over Christmas?

ICT
...that a computer can beat the world's best chess player?

Maths:
...that 6 x 7 = 42?

JUSTIFY

Give reason – Argue

Who has an argument for (doing) that?

What reasons could there be for believing this?

To justify means to offer reasons to back up what you believe, or what you have done or want to do, which is important when trying to persuade someone of something! These can't just be any reasons – they need to be ones that would be accepted as relevant and reasonable – so, not just a whim or an unconvincing excuse.

Say why
Excuse
Prove
Persuade

Reasons
Excuses
Grounds
Evidence
Position
Certainty
Proposition
Argument
Proof
Principles
Rationale
Valid

Rationality

Justify is a natural partner with **Infer** – almost the other side of the coin. To infer is to draw a conclusion from premises or reasons. To justify, on the other hand, is to **have drawn** a conclusion (or to have taken an action) and then to provide reasons for doing so. Doing it this way round is actually more common.

Without providing reasons, it's difficult to put a case to someone, let alone persuade them. Furthermore, by valuing reasons, learners will require good ones in order to be persuaded themselves. Habitually giving reasons also encourages learners to reflect on their own positions, double-checking that their views are based on solid reasoning.

It's also important that students understand that while 'everyone is entitled to their own opinion', the reasons for some opinions are stronger than for others and affect how much credibility those opinions have.

Crazy Reasons

This is a justification game in which players provide creative reasons for seemingly preposterous decisions. For example, one person in the pair says, *"I always take a hippo to the shops,"* and the other says, *"Of course! It can push people out of the way for you."* Then they swap and the other person initiates with an equally preposterous habit.

Why, Why, Why?

Pupils pair up. One person starts by saying something they genuinely believe. Their partner then asks *"Why?"*, and hears the reason. The partner continues to ask *"Why?"* in response to each reason until the first person can explain no further.

Second Why

This is a good teaching move or mindset. When a learner gives an answer followed by a reason, ask *"Why?"* a second time. In a philosophical discussion, they'll have to dig deeper inside themselves. If this is a lesson covering content, it requires them to make leaps and connections to other knowledge.

Facilitator/Facilitatee

When you have a substantial question to discuss in pairs, put up a PPT slide with:

Can you tell me more?
Can you say why?
So...? (repeat the question)
Can you give me an example?
How do you mean?
Why is that important?

One of the pair is the facilitator who uses only the questions on the slide to push the facilitatee's thinking deeper. Try to have a second substantial question ready, so that the pair can swap roles.

"Prepare your proof before you argue."
Jewish proverb

"Everywhere, authority and tradition have to justify themselves in the face of questions."
Gustav Heinemann

Applications:
Can you justify your opinion on...

English
...where the Iron Man came from?

History
...whether King John deserved his nickname?

Science
...whether all energy should be renewable?

KEYWORD

Highlight – Pinpoint

What are the key words in the lesson so far?

Can you highlight the key words in the text?

Sometimes it's easy for what is important to get lost in a mass of words. When you have a lot of information to process or remember, it's important to be able to pick out what's essential – the key words that capture the main ideas – or the ones that you're not sure of and need to understand.

Underline
Spotlight
Emphasise
Essentialise

Important
Main
Major
Basic
Central
Essential
Core
Fundamental
Theme
Emphases
Memorable
Significant

Acuteness

Tom remembers setting his students the task of highlighting key information of some text. Expecting sheets to come back with 10% of the words highlighted and 90% blank, he was surprised to see almost everyone had left 10% and highlighted 90%. He realised that, firstly, he assumed his students knew the criteria for what's worth highlighting and, secondly, his pupils were naturally risk averse to this kind of activity. If in doubt, they highlighted!

Whether or not you can relate to this in your teaching, it's crucial that we regularly give learners the chance to extract the essential ideas from information, so they can proceed to summarise effectively, either for themselves or for others.

Tom also taught a pupil who had an encyclopedic memory for the gory, quirky and humorous bits of history, but had no grasp of the big ideas and concepts involved. Fundamental to making progress is to understand and remember the big ideas, as everything else hangs off them like a clothes-line. Let's make sure they're remembering the right stuff!

Keyword Taboo

In pairs, students list five keywords as clues to any well-known film, book or TV programme. But it is not allowed ('taboo') for the list to contain any words from the film's title or any of its characters' names. Pairs join another, and each pair in turn reads the first of its keywords. Guesses are invited as to the title, and if they miss the mark then the second word is read out for further guesses and so on. The most successful pairs are those whose titles are guessed with the fourth or fifth keywords. An example is: 'Children, animals, adventures, making, ship = Blue Peter.'

Just 3 Words

To review a lesson or a discussion, call for students to write down JUST 3 WORDS to capture the essence of what they have learnt or discussed. These may be separate words, or in the form of a basic sentence. Then have a round of the class, each member giving a word each, checking off any that have already been said so as not to repeat them. If someone forms a three-word sentence, they should offer the whole sentence at once. This device may be used earlier in any lesson after a substantial exchange.

Panning for Gold

Panning for Gold involves rinsing a mix of materials so that the lighter, ordinary, unimportant stuff gets washed away, leaving only the heavier gold behind. Ask students to get rid of the less important words in a text so that only the important words, the 'gold' ones, are still visible. Keywording by elimination!

"Key words open the doors of understanding."
Roger Sutcliffe

Applications:
Panning for gold…

History
…in this description of Hitler's Germany?

English
…in Ron's letter to Harry?

PE
…in the instructions for trampolining?

LISTEN/LOOK

Notice – Gather

What do you see/hear/sense?
What have you gathered / found out?

Listening and looking are something we do so constantly we hardly notice the thinking involved. But careful listening and looking are crucial in learning and in understanding the world. Scientists notice things that other people haven't seen. Detectives pick up on small details of what people say in order to get to the truth. Other senses, such as smell, taste and touch, are also important.

Perceive
Observe
Apprehend
Make sense

Senses
Aware
Alert
Perception
Sensation
Sensitive
Observant
Environment
Information
Message
Communication
Mindful
Introspection

Attention
Comprehension

One of Art Costa's Habits of Mind is 'gathering data with all the senses'. This is a vital Thinking Move or habit because, if we are not careful, we can get lost in a world of ideas. Reminding ourselves to notice what is going on around us, or within us, keeps us in touch with the real world.

But it is not just raw data that we gather through our senses. When we hear words (or read them, by sight or touch) we are able to **make sense** of information or instruction that others are trying to communicate to us. And some information is so valuable to us that we actively seek it out, in books or elsewhere. In other words, Listen/Look can be as advanced a move as researching.

Finally, numerous studies attest to the benefits of attending to our inner world and training ourselves to keep calm or mindful in a world of rolling news, notifications and (social) networking. There is also a sense in which we may listen to our intuitions or gut feelings – which can be as important a move as listening to reasons and arguments, especially when we come to **Weigh up**.

Attention!

There is a world of difference between randomly looking **around** and deliberately looking **for** something, with senses attuned to a particular objective. Ask the class to look around the room. Then give the name of a colour and ask students to look around again. What did they notice the second time but not the first? It's remarkable how even tiny details stand out.

Resting Receptors

Ask students to sit comfortably and close their eyes. Explain that they are to use their senses to follow your instructions, in silence, in their head. How many different sounds can they hear? What are their aches and pains? Are they sitting comfortably? Does their last meal still linger on their taste-buds? How long does each breath last? After a few minutes, let them share their answers with a partner and then with the group.

Did I miss something?

Player A speaks to Player B for 90 seconds on a true story or the current topic of study. B must then verbally recall to A as much as he or she remembers. When they have recalled all they can, B asks, *"Did I miss something?"* Player A reminds them of anything they've missed. If it's about the topic under study, Player A can then also ask, *"Did I miss something?"* with B supplying missing details.

"You see, but you do not observe. The distinction is clear."
Sherlock Holmes in A. C. Doyle's *A Scandal in Bohemia*

Applications:
Did I miss something?
An excellent revision tool for storylines and processes:

English
What happens in Romeo and Juliet?

Science
What happens in the water cycle?

RE
What are the elements of a Passover meal and what do they mean?

MAINTAIN

Believe – Afﬁrm

Who agrees with that statement?
Could someone take a position on this?

To maintain a belief is to hold that it is true or valuable. It is not just having a belief but consciously committing to it. We may do this privately, i.e. without telling anyone, but if we do make our belief public, someone may Test or doubt it. In that case, we would probably need to Justify it. Or maybe it is someone else's belief that is being doubted but we agree with it. Then if we declare our support for their position, that would be another form of maintaining.

Agree
Support
Hold
Assert

Belief
Claim
True
Reality
Position
Point of view
Committed
Convinced
Value
Principle
Worldview
Axiom

Conviction

There are pastoral as well as academic benefits to developing students' ability to maintain. Pastorally, we don't want them to 'follow their friends', but think for themselves and act with integrity. We should therefore encourage them to maintain or assert their point of view, especially if it might differ from their friends' or the majority's. We should also encourage them to praise and support others who may be in a minority – a move that's reportedly becoming rarer in the workplace.

Academically, we want students to have the confidence to take a position and be ready to defend or justify it. Without this intellectual challenge, we run the risk of developing compliant students who are neither critical nor creative. It is also important that they learn to recognise when someone else is taking a position – which is not always obvious – and then to position themselves in response.

True or False?
A simple game to help students be clear when someone is making a 'truth claim'. You or the pupils can make up statements for a quiz or find examples on the Internet.

Change Places If (Contestable Statements)
Put students in a circle or horseshoe. Stand in the middle, with no spare seats available, and say, *"Change places if you believe that girls are better students than boys"*, or some such contestable statement. Ask students holding the minority belief to stand at a distance from each other in the middle of the circle. Invite those who remain seated, one at a time, to stand with someone in the middle. Make sure everyone standing has a pair before everyone else joins a group. Tell students to justify their position in their small groups before they sit down again. Emphasise that the belief you put forward was contestable – a 'value judgement'. Ask students to agree, in pairs, on two value judgements they think others will disagree with. Invite a volunteer to swap places with you and complete *"Change places if you believe …"* with a contestable statement of their own, making sure they go to sit in someone else's place. A new student should be left to offer a contestable statement. Let everyone have fun changing places, but pause for discussion if the belief is particularly contestable.

Bracketing Beliefs
Give students a text, from a text book or newspaper, and ask them to bracket off each assertion or truth claim. You can model this, showing that some sentences contain more than one assertion, and that some assertions are not truth claims but opinions. If the latter, they should also be underlined. (Some sentences will be instructions not assertions.) When students have finished, ask them to count the pairs of brackets. Do they all agree on the number? Are some assertions more questionable than others?

"I maintain that nothing useful and lasting can emerge from violence."
Shirin Ebadi

"If you don't stand for something you will fall for anything."
Gordon A. Eadie

Applications:
Change places if you think…

English
…'devious' is the most accurate word to describe Fagan

Music
…this piece of music fits into the Baroque genre

History
…numbers was the biggest factor in William conquering Norman England?

NEGATE

Disagree – Oppose

Does anyone disbelieve what X says?
Does anyone disagree with Y's position?

This move is the opposite of **Maintain**. Here, we express our disagreement with someone, perhaps denying the truth or value of their claim, or the relevance or validity of their argument. People can shy away from disagreeing with others, but disagreeing with someone is a way of respecting them and taking their ideas seriously, especially when you make clear that it's the idea you are disagreeing with rather than the person.

Disagree
Object
Deny
Dispute

Disagree
Wrong
False
Negative
Opposite
Contrary
Counter
Contradiction
Denial
Rebuttal
Challenge
Antithesis

Opposition

At its most effective, negation is done by producing a counter-example or even a whole counter-argument. But it may also be done by simply contradicting or by offering an alternative account or perspective. It's arguably the basis of critical thinking.

Helping students feel comfortable disagreeing with one another, and not feel personally under attack when their ideas are challenged, is crucial for open discussion. Artificial debates with students assigned to one side or another can be helpful, though skill in argument should never be valued or cultivated more than sincerity. Terms like those in the left column ensure that discussions are focused on a clash of ideas, rather than of personality.

But What If...?

This paired game is a good way to practice the focused turn-taking involved in negation – and reassertion, which is sort of negation of negation! It's easiest explained with an example:

A: What if you wanted to know the time?
B: I'd look at my phone.
A: But what if your phone was out of battery?
B: I'd charge it up.
A: But what if you'd lost your charger?
B: I'd use someone else's.
A: But what if there was a power cut?
B: I'd use the clock in the school hall?
A: But what if the power cut lasted so long, all
    the batteries had run out?
B: I'd see when the sun came up.

What if you wanted to meet the Queen?
What if you wanted to go to sleep?
What if you wanted to eat some ice cream?

Disagreement Duet

Pair up with a friend. Find as many things as possible that you disagree about in 147 seconds. Afterwards, choose one and try to persuade the other to change their mind.

Brainstand

During a discussion, get everyone to do a Brainstand, swapping sides and arguing the opposite to what they believe. Standing physically on opposing sides helps to turn the discussion into more of a game.

"Without contraries there is no progression."
William Blake

Applications:
Who has a counterargument / counter-example to...

Philosophy
...what Annie just said?

Science
...the view that science can explain everything?

Maths
...the working out of this equation?

ORDER

Sequence – Arrange

Let's put these things into an order...
Do we need a plan for this?

Things can be put into order in time (e.g. events into a sequence), or in space (places mapped out, furniture arranged), or in any other order that makes things easier to think about and deal with – from largest to smallest, most certain to most doubtful, best to worst. You could even order ways of ordering things from the most to the least useful.

Line up
Timetable
Lay out
Map

First/Next
Step/Stage
Series
Timetable
Plan
Method
System
Procedure
Line
Layout
Map
Coordinates

Orderliness

Students often don't get as much practice in this move as they might, as we tend to do a lot of the organising and planning for them. We have to be willing to have some chaos at the start for them to bring some order to!

As well as arranging things in time and space, ordering can be about ranking things in order of magnitude, importance, usefulness, beauty, impact – or many other concepts, objective or contestable. Ranking or prioritising helps students to be resourceful and keep on top of their own work and life-loads.

Having everything ordered for you makes for an easy life, but it's also disempowering. We can help students become self-organisers by eschewing micro-management – instead encouraging them to set their own goals and allowing them to choose the means and plan the steps to achieving them.

How to Make...

Place two slices of bread, jam, butter and a butter-knife on your desk. Ask pairs or threes to produce a sequence of instructions to enable a robot to make a jam sandwich with them. After 5–10 minutes, let students read their instructions while you follow their commands as a non-thinking robot would, to inevitable hilarity! Other simple activities that require methodical steps are making a cup of tea or cleaning your teeth. Students could present each other with similar challenges.

Order, Order, Order!

For any 'group of things' you've encountered in the curriculum, get students to write each on a piece of paper. Ask them to put them into an order (of their own choosing) and when done, invite a neighbouring group to guess what the thinking behind the order is. This can be repeated with different orders and groups challenging each other.

First Moves First

Before any given project or piece of work, ask learners what move they think needs to be made first. Once one is agreed, ask someone to stand in a space to represent that move. Ask what would be needed next, and the person representing it puts their hand on the shoulder of the first. Continue the process, creating a planned sequence of moves for the task ahead.

"Good order is the foundation of all things."
Edmund Burke

Applications:
Put these into an order...

Music
Brass instruments

History
Victorian inventions

Science
Features of the rainforest

PICTURE

Imagine – Put yourself

Let's picture the scene...
Put yourself in the scene / shoes of...

Sometimes you can make better sense of things or ideas by trying hard to picture them, as in a movie. You can even put yourself into the picture – imagining that you are in somebody else's shoes, trying to see what they would see and feel what they would feel.

Visualise
Conjure up
Pretend
Immerse yourself

Scene/Scenario
Mind's eye
Representation
Image
Vision
Model
Projection
Make believe
Daydream
Immersion
In their shoes / place
Empathy

Imagination

To picture is to see something in the mind's eye, and this move has many uses. One is to ensure that your thinking is precise and concrete. If you cannot picture something with clarity and detail, you may overlook a significant aspect of it. Before you buy a sofa, you do well to visualise (as well as **Size**) your living room.

Another use is 'envisioning' the future, a vital aspect of creativity, which involves imagining things other than as they are. Visualising your future self is also a common technique in sports psychology and can help raise aspirations. It's also potentially a rich experience for imaginative immersion in a topic area, particularly using prior learning to visualise the world of a text or historical era.

Yet another important use is that of imagining yourself in another's shoes. It is a cognitive move, certainly, but it could be seen as a moral move, too – one that most moves us to feel empathy and display compassion towards others (as well as sharing in their happiness).

What's in Your Picture?

Practise firstly with the whole group, asking everyone to picture an object, such as a car, in their mind's eye. Emphasise that you want them to visualise their object as fully and clearly as they can. Then ask them questions of detail, such as, *"What colour is the car in your picture?"* or *"Does it have an aerial?"* (It doesn't matter if the student has not visualised any particular detail. The richness of people's visual pictures and capacity to hold them in mind varies widely: it's an interesting internal difference.) Then students play in pairs. One visualises an object or scene (either one known to them, or an imaginary / 'typical' one) and the other asks questions of detail and tries to re-imagine or copy their partner's image. After a while, the partners reverse their roles. This game is particularly valuable in History and Literature.

Mind's I

Using a picture that includes a human character within the context under study, ask students to look at the picture and fix its details in their memory. Then ask them to close their eyes and imagine they are the person in the picture. What can they see? What can they hear? What do they feel? What are they thinking? What one line of words are they saying to themselves? They can then return to their classroom selves and share what their lines of internal monologue were in pairs and onwards to the class.

Picture Perfect?

Students sit back to back, each with two pieces of blank A4, on one of which each does a drawing (not too simple, not too complex). Each in turn describes their drawing to their partner, who tries to replicate it on their blank sheet. The descriptions should not include the names of any drawn items but may name shapes or similar items. Pictures are compared at the end.

"Imagination is more important than knowledge. It encircles the world."
Albert Einstein

"Formulate and stamp indelibly on your mind a mental picture of yourself as succeeding. Hold this picture tenaciously. Never permit it to fade. Your mind will seek to develop the picture... Do not build up obstacles in your imagination."
Norman Vincent Peale

Applications:
In your mind, picture...

History
...Rosa Parks as she took her seat on the bus

Art
...Van Gogh as he painted the café at night

Maths
...what a 2D world is like

QUESTION

Ask – Wonder

What questions could we ask about this?
Let's get into wonder mode...

In school, you spend a lot of time answering teachers' questions. But to enjoy learning independently, you need to ask questions yourself. Questioning is important for practical things, such as getting information and advice, but also for the pleasure of being curious. (Could scientists ever genetically engineer a unicorn?) It also helps you work out if the things other people tell you are actually true! (Is playing video games really bad for your brain?)

Inquire
Investigate
Puzzle
Problematise

Where, when, etc.
Open/Closed
Puzzle
Problem
Awe
Mystery
Empirical
(Re)search
Conceptual
Inquiry
Leading
Rhetorical

Inquisitiveness

Questioning is a skill at which young students excel but which can fade as childhood progresses into adolescence. Learners need to develop the will, as well as the skills, to inquire. This comes through practice: developing questioning as a regular habit, but also celebrating spontaneous questioning.

Sometimes a teacher might respond with an encouragement (or better still, some time) to do some private research. At other times, with a probing question of her own, the teacher encourages and empowers pupils to think things through for themselves.

Questioning in the classroom is notoriously dominated by teachers, not pupils, and a vital message of the *Thinking Moves* A–Z is to encourage pupils to think independently. Every move is, in effect, the answer to a question. It is good if a pupil gives a thoughtful answer to a teacher's question. It is better still if they stimulate their own thinking by asking themselves more questions.

Question Chain
Partners take turns asking each other questions, aiming to link them all in a chain by ensuring that at least one word from one question appears in the next one. Importantly, the 'question' word in one question (e.g. when, how, is, could) should NOT start the next one. This rule ensures a greater variety of questions. Pairs write down their questions and choose the most interesting chain of three to read out.

Four Wonders For
This can be used at any time in a topic or unit but the earlier the better. Ask students to each come up with four *"I wonder…?"* statements about the topic. These should be four things they are curious about and to which they don't know the answer.

Ask Me A Question
Turn the tables and get the students to ask you questions about the topic. Don't ask, *"Does anyone have a question?"* – you probably won't get any. Ask, *"Could everyone write down three questions to ask me: the one you think will be most helpful to your learning about this topic; the one you think is the most interesting; and one you think will be difficult to answer but worth answering."* Write them on whiteboards, pick some to answer and show you don't know everything, enlisting their help. It's a good way of showing vulnerability and curiosity.

"There is more to be learned from the unexpected questions of children than from the discourses of men."
John Locke

Applications:
Give me four wonders for…

History
…the Romans (e.g. why was their army so strong?)

Science
…plants (e.g. can plants survive in space?)

Maths
…numbers (e.g. what's the biggest number?)

RESPOND

Answer – Reply

Who has a response to that?
Is that an answer to the question?

People often say you should live life to the full. Usually, they are encouraging others to take opportunities to go places or pursue some activity. But part of getting the most out of life is responding with interest to what is going on around you. It is good to be an active listener and observer, but it is better still to respond with an answer or at least with an expression of interest.

React
Remark
Feed back
Comment

(Dis)Like
Made me
(I) Think
Reaction
Feeling
Emotional
Opinion
Comment
Personal
Subjective
View
Value

Responsiveness

One of the regular complaints of teachers is that some of their pupils are passive learners: they are not interested in 'learning' other than what they have to know for tests or exams. At its worst, this is the opposite – even the nadir – of education.

Good teachers manage to stir the interest of their students in their subject, and the best teachers are those who stir interest in the relationship between their subject and the project of humanity. But how can this be done?

There might be as many answers to this question as good teachers, but one simple thing might link them all: **showing interest in what interests students.** This is not a facile interest in student pastimes – though that could sometimes be the basis for a growing, intellectual relationship. It is rather a matter of modelling a constructive response to any responses that students make to the subject matter in hand: asking probing questions or encouraging conceptual connections to be made. In short, it is about dialogical, or philosophical, teaching – see
www.philosophicalteaching.com

Yes, and ... Yes, but

One student in a pair starts with a statement 'of the moment' – perhaps an observation, a recollection, or a point of view. The partner must respond, beginning, *"Yes, and ...."* and finishing with a complementary statement. The first student, in turn, responds with, *"Yes, and ...."* and so on. An alternative or additional format is for the response to begin, *"Yes, but ...."* An interesting difference between the two sorts of responses can emerge when students reflect on their conversations.

Sentence Sharing

One student in a pair gives one word to start a sentence, e.g. 'Yesterday' or 'Sometimes'. The partner gives the next word, the first student the third – alternating words but with the aim of finishing the sentence with the 10th word. Ideally, students count the words on their fingers. Sentences can turn out to be fairly plain or quite surreal. The point is to respond constructively to each other.

All Hands on Deck

Discussions are more thoughtful and go deeper when students respond to one another rather than make isolated points directed at the teacher. In a discussion, ask everyone to respond to a point made by indicating if they agree or disagree. Better than thumbs up or down is to have hands on the table for agreement, under the table for disagreement. Some will discover that one hand on the table and one under can stand for *"I agree and disagree"*. Then you can hear the reasons why people agree or disagree with the statement.

"Life is a gift, and I try to respond with grace and courtesy."
Maya Angelou

Applications:
All hands on deck...

Maths
Is Julie's answer correct?

History
Martin has said Henry VIII was a bad man but a good king. Do we agree?

Art
Usamaah thinks his work doesn't need anything more. What we do we think?

SIZE

Estimate – Quantify

Could we try to put a figure on how many?
Are you saying all, or most, or just some?

There will be many occasions when you need to know, roughly, the number, amount or size of something. To do this you need to quantify. Quantifying may be calculating exactly, or just making a good estimate so you've a good idea of how many of something there are. If you are not careful, you can make big mistakes – not ordering enough food for a party, for example!

Count
Measure
Reckon
Figure

All/No(ne)
Some/Most
Few/Many
Number
Amount
Frequency
Fraction
Proportion
Majority/minority
Scale
Degree
Continuum

Sense of proportion

'Getting the measure of something', or 'sizing up the task' is essential for planning ahead. Estimating how much equipment you will need, or how long a task might take, is a routine part of most practical projects. Reckoning how much the average person might eat, and how much it might cost, informs how much of a party budget goes on food. Computing how long a journey might determine which mode of transport is taken or whether you stop overnight.

There is also a clear value to students in deliberately practising this move at school. Estimating how long this week's homework might take will impact on their efficiency (as well as what social plans can be made). Reckoning how long to spend on each question in a test can pay dividends. And, of course, the more advanced most studies get, the more students need to appreciate the significance of statistical data.

Figure it Out

Making reasonable estimates of quantities is a useful skill. This can be as simple as guessing the number of marbles in a jar or estimating the number of chairs in the school. For older students, as a greater challenge, you can create a 'Fermi question', named after the educated guesswork the famous physicist used to estimate the chances of intelligent life elsewhere in the universe. For example:

How many Camembert cheeses are there in France?
How many Maths teachers are there in the UK?
How many goals were scored in the Premier League last year?

All or Nothing

Introduce students to the form of logical (strictly, Aristotelian) statements: 'All/Some/No *A*s are/have *B*s' and offer a first example: 'All trees have leaves'. Invite a next statement beginning 'Some / No leaves', e.g. 'No leaves are made of metal,' and then, e.g. 'Some metals are used to make coins.'

Rule 1: the quantifier (All/Some/No) must change each time.

Rule 2: the rest of the sentence must contain a noun, which can then be re-used in the next statement. The game can be played in groups of any size.

A Number to Think of

You can generate curiosity and engagement around any topic by giving a number that is connected to the topic in some way and asking what it's the number of.

"Measure twice, cut once."
Proverbial advice

Applications:
Number to think of

Geography
13mm (average growth of a stalactite)

Chemistry
450 million (tonnes of fertilizer produced using the Haber process annually)

Maths
23,249,425 (number of digits of the largest prime number discovered as of July 2018)

TEST

Doubt – Check

Is there any reason to doubt this claim?
Let's check the assumptions/facts!

Not all ideas are good ones, and it is often wise to put them to the test – that is, to check whether they are well based or well thought through. Just like a spelling test tests how good at spelling you are, to 'test' an idea means to see how good it is.

Put in question
Make sure
Challenge
Examine

Doubtful
Claim
Really
Sure
Questionable
Assumption
Bias
Checklist
Mistake(n)
Testimony
Reliable
Confirmation

Scepticism

There are different sorts of ideas, and they can be tested in different ways. One main sort is beliefs about the world – what we claim or **Maintain** to be true. These are usually tested or challenged by calling for evidence or simply by checking the facts, including assumptions, for oneself.

This is a move that might be particularly encouraged in budding scientists, but it is not the prerogative only of scientists. In fact, it is a practice that should be encouraged in every subject and in everyday life. Careful testing remains the bulwark against false gossip, urban myths and, of course, fake news!

Another important sort of idea is a value judgment – not so much a claim about how the world is as about how it ought to be, or what we value and try to promote. When we 'test for value', we are not primarily calling for facts but for justifications – of principles, proposals, opinions. We don't assess these for their truth, but on a scale from the strongest possible reason to extremely weak ones.

How Would You Test?

Come up with a range of statements that can be tested for truth. They can be both fantastical and factual – the important thing is they are beyond everyday experience. In pairs, get students to suggest how they would carry on the test, step by step. Examples: *"How would you test... if there were an edge to our universe? ...if unicorns once existed? ...if aliens had abducted you last night and put you in a classroom simulation?"*

Lie Detector

A development of True or False (see **Maintain**). At the beginning of any new topic, give students two statements, one true, one false, or one statement that can be either true or false. Ask them to pair up and work out how they would test which is true and which is false. What information would they need? What questions would they ask? You might even set them the task of finding out the answers.

Verify/Falsify

Put a range of true and false statements on the board. Ask students to work through them, using their knowledge to either *Verify* (prove it to be true) or *Falsify* (prove it to be false), showing their working in each case. If they cannot verify or falsify, they should explain why and outline what could assist them, or how they might assess or size the degree of probability. They could also argue that the statement is a value judgement and therefore neither verifiable nor falsifiable.

"Good tests kill flawed theories; we remain alive to guess again."
Karl Popper

Applications:
How would you test...

Geography
...if Brazil's economy is thriving

Maths
...which of these equations is correct?

Music
...if the moods music creates are natural or learned

USE

Try Out – Apply

Who can see a use for this?
Let's put this into practice!

If an idea looks like a good one, then it makes sense to put it into practice, otherwise you might as well not have had it. This means looking out for the opportunity to use it – and taking that opportunity!

Try out
Put to use
Experiment
Implement

Practical
Experiment
(In) practice
(in) action
Effective
Application
Function
Utility
Purpose
Implementation
Transfer
Imitation

Pragmatism

Whatever we do with our minds can be put to good use. It might be knowing something that helps us navigate our way through the world, or a skill that can be applied in various contexts once mastered. Or it might be an idea or principle arrived at from discussion that can then be put into action, such as following through on a discussion about freedom of speech by supporting a charity for imprisoned journalists.

Of course, learning needs to be put to use inside the classroom too. Knowledge and skills can fade and rust if they're not regularly applied. We should ensure that students devote enough of their lesson time to demonstrating, transferring and using what they've taken on. The question we, and they, might continually be asking is: *"How can we apply this understanding?"*

Message in Your Pocket
Each student writes down on a piece of paper a message to themself which they think would be useful to remember during the week. It could be something about how to act, how to think, how to feel. They then fold the paper up small, and keep it close to them, e.g. in a back pocket, to remind them of their intention. At the end of the week, ask them to think about whether and when they used their Message in a Pocket. For best results, do this exercise yourself with something the week before, and share the result with them beforehand.

Who and How?
At the end of any period of study (could be a lesson or a whole unit), ask students to reflect on the skills and knowledge they have developed. Who in the outside world would use this? How would they use it? This not only helps them think about applications and uses, but it also helps them appreciate the relevance of what they are learning (and might provide some careers advice by stealth!).

So, What?
At the end of a discussion (about a problem facing us or about the rights and wrongs of something), it would seem a waste of time and energy if we then go back to business as usual. End a discussion by asking the class *"So, what?"* and let them suggest applications of principles and conclusions they've arrived at.

Choose a Move
Help learners practise thinking about other Thinking Moves in a fun and fantastical way. Present them with a scenario, such as below, asking what Thinking Move they would need to make ...
...if there was a power shortage so that there was only electricity for three hours each day?
...if they discovered they had shrunk to the size of a Lego person?
...if they won a million pounds but had to spend it all within one week?

"The great end of life is not knowledge but action."
Francis Bacon

Applications:
So, what...

Geography
...will you do to reduce plastic pollution?

PSHE
...will you do to help new students settle in?

Art
...will you do to incorporate Impressionism into your work?

VARY

Change – Alter

Is there a better way of doing this?
Does anyone have an alternative idea/perspective?

Sometimes we all just get stuck. We know things are not working out, but we don't know what we should do about it. A very good next move, then, is quite simply to try something different!

Play with
Adapt
Modify
Diversify

Different
(An) other
Way
Perspective
Instead
Alternative
Version
Extra
Substitution
Modification
Adaptation
Trial and error

Adaptability

Vary is a prime creative Thinking Move. It can be made at the everyday level of striving to improve whatever one is doing – including what one is saying or writing. 'www.ebi' – 'what went well, even better if' is a good strategy for this. Or it can be made at the more entrepreneurial level of trying to come up with radically new ideas.

A great example of this in pedagogy is Pie Corbett's Imitate, Innovate, Invent approach to writing: first becoming familiar with a text, and then varying elements of it, before more independent writing. It's an important contribution to undoing the bad press that 'copying' traditionally has in schools.

Varying can involve a trial-and-error approach, i.e. trying different things and seeing how well they work – 'playing around' with an idea. Or it can involve rethinking an approach – 'thinking laterally' – most famously done by the likes of Darwin and Dyson. Either way, varying discourages learners from settling with their first answer or idea.

New Choice!

A paired storytelling game. One player starts telling a story. At any time, their partner can call, *"New choice!"* and the last thing said or done must be changed.

A: Once upon a time there was a boy...
B: New Choice!
A: Once upon a time there was a girl...
B: New Choice!
A: Once upon a time there was a hippo. He had lots of hippo friends who liked wallowing in the mud...
B: New Choice!

Socrates' Sieve

1. Start with a proverb or popular opinion, such as, *"It's wrong to hurt people."*
2. Find an exception where it doesn't work (*"A nurse giving an injection"*).
3. Restate the principle with qualifiers that allow for the exception (*"It's wrong to hurt people unless you are doing it for their own good"*).
4. See if there is an exception to the restated principle (*"A parent spanking a child"*).
5. Repeat the process until you have a principle that covers all situations.

Give Us Another!

This can be used after asking any question that has several possible, valid answers and is a playful way to stretch confident speakers. Ask a question and if such a student answers, fire back, *"Give us another!"* and keep going until they run out of alternative answers. The answers must be correct (they can't just give wrong ones) and if there are still right answers that remain unsaid, invite others to *"Give us another!"*

"When we are no longer able to change a situation, we are challenged to change ourselves."
Viktor E. Frankl

"Change your life today. Don't gamble on the future, act now, without delay."
Simone de Beauvoir

Applications:
Give us another...

Geography
physical process

Technology
way to cut wood

History
consequence of the slave trade

WEIGH UP

Decide – Judge

Let's weigh up the pros and cons for this.
So, what has been decided?

This is what you do, or least should do, whenever you make a decision – weigh up the reasons for and against something. Some choices are obvious, but others can be close calls that take a lot of careful thinking about pros and cons.

Choose
Assess
Evaluate
Deliberate

Good/Bad
Best/Worst
Right/Wrong
(Would you) Rather
Decision
Pros/Cons
Dilemma
Balance
Impartial
Considerations
Criteria
Verdict

Judiciousness

It's no coincidence that the most common symbol for judging is old-fashioned scales. The scales vividly represent how we weigh up the evidence on each side of a dispute, or the pros and cons of a decision, to reach a balanced judgment. That can be through objective measurement or complex, often subjective, criteria. Of course, deciding what criteria to use is itself a matter of judgement, as is deciding which criteria are the most important.

To judge is to be aware that not all answers are obvious. Some questions are contestable, and so their answers won't (and shouldn't) be provided by the teacher. Most formal assessments require independent conclusions to be drawn, but judging is important beyond the exam hall. Wise decisions are needed in personal and professional lives about what is true, what is right, and what to do. These involve careful thought and consideration of our own biases too.

Good Idea, Bad Idea

Divide your space in half with a skipping rope. Ask a contestable question, e.g. *"Zoos for animals – good idea or bad idea?"* Ask everyone to move to the 'good idea' side. Get students to pair and share reasons to support the idea. It's like a shoal of fish – safety in numbers! Don't hear back from the pairs or you'll steal the thunder of the final step.

Then move everyone to the 'bad idea' side, and do the same with the reasons against. Finally ask them the question again, and let them show what they think now by standing on the side of their choice. Now is the time for some to share their reasons with the whole group, because they have had a chance to safely rehearse what they might say. The same activity, with a suitable question, helps teenagers working on argumentative writing, or you can use it to liven up a longer philosophical enquiry.

Pro-Con Processor

Gather reasons for and against something. Then focus on the 'pros', and ask what the strongest reason is on that side of the argument and why. Continue ranking reasons from strongest to weakest, voting if necessary. Repeat with the 'cons'. The point of doing each side separately is that students often struggle to separate consideration of the strength of a reason from whether or not they agree with the conclusion it supports.

Find your MoJO

As indicated in thinking **Back**, deliberate reflection is a bedrock of good learning, even at the level of memorising facts. Deep learning or understanding, though, is promoted by **doing** something with the facts you can remember. So, plan or be ready to seize Moments of Judgement or Opinion, asking students to make a **decision** based on the facts that they can remember (or will, when they start thinking about the decision).

"A wise person apportions their belief with the evidence."
David Hume

"Every man must decide whether he will walk in the light of creative altruism or in the darkness of destructive selfishness."
Martin Luther King, Jr.

Applications:
Pro-con Processor

Geography
Siting of a settlement

RE
Responses to the problem of evil

History
Was revolution in Russia inevitable?

eXEMPLIFY

Give Example – Illustrate

Can you give an example of that?
Does anyone have a counter-example?

The more complex an idea, the more helpful it can be to give a specific example. It's easier to understand stars by thinking about our own sun. Examples can also be used to strengthen and oppose arguments. People themselves can be thought of as examples. Rosa Parks is often held up as giving an example of courage.

Say (for instance)
Give an instance
Cite
Instantiate

Example
Real life
Event
Experience
Instance
Scenario
Case study
Typical
Sample
Exemplar
Specimen
Citation

Groundedness

Education often proceeds by getting students to understand general principles via memorable examples. How often do you **Explain** something in the abstract to someone, to be met with a blank expression, before you say *'for example...'* in the hope the penny drops? Examples tie general ideas into specific experience. If we want learners to manage their learning, we should encourage them to think of their own examples.

Examples are crucial not only for understanding but for argument too. In discussions, an example often brings the question to life. It can sometimes be persuasive, but it can equally ignite a lively exchange – especially when it features people or is viewed in different ways. One example often leads to another, perhaps even a counter-example, and that opens up the opportunity for other Thinking Moves such as to **Connect** or **Divide** the scenarios.

Example Chain

This paired game makes use of the way the same thing can be an example of two or more general kinds. A asks the questions, B answers:

A: Think of a thing.
B: A seagull.
A: What kind of thing is that?
B: A bird.
A: What's another example of a bird?
B: An eagle.
A: What kind of thing is that? (you can't say 'bird')
B: A predator.
A: What's another example of a predator?
B: A tiger.
A: What kind of thing is that?

They can swap roles and share some of the chains of examples and kinds created.

Yes, No, Maybe

For any concept under discussion, ask for something they think is an example of it, something they think is not, and something which is a borderline case they're not sure of. It is these last grey examples that provoke the most disagreement and richest discussion.

Needs – Yes, water; no, Xbox; maybe, electricity
Sports – Yes, football; no, baking; maybe, dancing

Best Example

Some things can be held up as paradigms or exemplars of a class or concept. For example, dogs might be regarded as the best example of pets, or London of multicultural cities. Not everyone will agree on a choice, and an interesting discussion could arise as to what criteria are or should be used. Perhaps most interesting could be discussions about exemplary people (leaders, sportspeople, teachers, students).

"The road to learning by precept is long, but by example short and effective."
Seneca

Applications:
Give us a Yes, No, Maybe for...

Dance
...a performance

ICT
...a robot

Art
...an artwork

YIELD

Accept – Concede

Has anyone changed their mind?
What part of their argument can you accept?

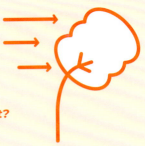

You yield when you give way to someone else by, at least, stopping to let them speak. But you yield all the more when you adjust your ideas to theirs. You may even go so far as to change your mind – which you should usually regard as a good thing to do.

Come around to
Admit
Accommodate
Compromise

Having heard
On second thoughts
Maybe
Negotiation
Compromise
Deal
Adjustment
Concession
Change of mind
Synthesis
Self-correction
Reconciliation

Flexibility

The decision to stop holding one belief or position and accept another is clearly a significant move of thought and, often, a collaborative one. It can also be desirable, especially when there is good evidence or argument to warrant a change of mind.

The pity is that humans do not always find it easy to accept when they need to change their minds. They become more attached to 'their' ideas than to seeking the truth, although perhaps they just need to save face.

Cultivating a flexibility to see merit in others' ideas, reconcile and reconstruct is a good balance to the habit of 'always stick to what you believe'. A teacher might point to the drift of an argument and ask an individual, gently, if they would be willing to yield some ground. They could also use the language of compromise, pointing out the need sometimes to see a situation from another point of view and be willing to negotiate.

I Used to Think... Now I Think...
Ask students in pairs to share something they used to believe, but which they no longer believe. What was it that changed their minds? Gather some of the reasons for the changing beliefs and see what they have in common.

All in All
Ask students individually to list some generalisations – things that they believe are generally true, but which might have some exceptions – with space beneath each one. Next, ask them to think up possible exceptions and add them to the space below. The same activity can be done with suggestions for new laws, and when they would accept them being broken.

Common Ground
This move can be used during or after any debate between two sides. Get each side to identify Common Ground with the other. Good questions to invite this are:

What do you agree on?
Where do you accept the other side is right?
What do you concede?

These questions help students realise that one can concede a point without conceding an argument. In each one, the language of the question assumes there is an answer. They can still say, *"Nothing! They're wrong about everything!"* but the door is open to yielding.

"When the facts change, I change my mind. What do you do, sir?"
Originally attributed to John Maynard Keynes, but we have to concede its origin is unknown!

Applications:
Common Ground...

RS
(Abortion): The Pro Choice side might agree with Pro Life that abortion is a tragedy.

History
The defence team for Charles I might admit that he has made several mistakes.

Geography
Those arguing for drastic measures to prevent climate disaster might concede that some people might have to give up more than others.

ZOOM

Focus on – Survey

In: What should we focus on now?
Out: Let's step back and look at the big picture

When directors make films, they use different camera shots for different purposes. They might zoom in to show the sweat on the brow of a hero at a tense moment or zoom out to show the full scale of an army ready for battle. In thinking, zooming in on details and zooming out to get the bigger picture can both be important.

Inspect
Scrutinise
Review
Take stock

Focus
Detail
Particular
Tiny
Aspect
Perspective
Big picture
Overview
General
System
Pattern
Gestalt

Concentration
Comprehensiveness

Zooming in means giving closer attention to the small details. Zooming out shows things in proportion or perspective. The journal of a single soldier or a map of the front can both be illuminating in understanding a conflict. You can zoom in or out in time as well: what makes news today is rarely as important as trends that develop over years and decades.

Choosing the best level at which to investigate something is part of being a good inquirer. You might need to focus on a particular word to understand the question better, but you should also step back occasionally to **Weigh up** how well your inquiry is going.

In Science, seeing how different levels fit together is especially important to understanding complex systems, e.g. seeing how processes within individual cells connect to bodily movements. Stepping back can also help you spot patterns, which may be significant in History, or Art, as well as in Science.

S,M,H,D,W,M,Y,D,C,M

First solve the puzzle of what this series means – units of time from second to millennium. Then consider something broad and interesting – the life of an animal, or a nation. Think about what might be important in understanding it at each of these timescales – from respiration to natural selection, or from the signing of a treaty to the preservation of a language.

Yo-yo Facilitation

Move from a particular question, such as, *"Was it right for the UK to go to war over Czechoslovakia?"* to a more general question, such as, *"When is it right to go to war?"* and back again, using the particular arguments to inform general principles and vice versa. (Also see the Hokey-Kokey Method from the Philosophy Foundation.)

Gradual Picture Reveal

Start with a small detail from a picture to get focused attention and invite predictions as you gradually reveal the whole thing.

Half-Time Oranges

At some point through a project or piece of work (it doesn't have to be mid-way), ask learners to pause and consider which Thinking Moves they have made so far and which would be most helpful to do next. You could go a step further by asking which have been easiest or hardest, and activate some members of the class to act as 'Move Mentors' for others.

"That's been one of my mantras – focus and simplicity."
Steve Jobs

"See what happens if you step back instead of bounding forward."
Nora Roberts

Applications:
Yo-yo facilitation

Geography
Is salmon farming sustainable? What makes something sustainable?

English
Is Jekyll and Hyde a typical Gothic novel? What makes a Gothic novel?

Biology
Are bacteria parasites? What makes something a parasite?

THINKING GROOVES

These are sequences of Thinking Moves that can become Thinking Grooves – established routines or habits for some common classroom tasks. This idea is similar to Ron Ritchhart's handy Thinking Routines but with significant differences.

One is that his routines are not essentially sequences of moves, although some of them are, more or less. (Actually, he conceives of Thinking Moves differently anyway – more like general strategies than particular acts of thinking.)

Another is that there is a huge potential range of Thinking Grooves, given that they consist of three-move combinations, with 26 basic moves to choose from. Our concept of the Thinking Grooves, then, is not only that there might be ones that are fit for regular use in everyday or academic activities, but also that individuals can themselves invent and implement combinations. Thinking Moves thus provides a sort of do-it-yourself toolkit for more thoughtful activity.

Here are a few suggested Thinking Grooves for academic use. If any teacher invents and uses a new groove for a particular subject or topic, we would be pleased to hear of it and to post it, with due credit, on our website!

Planning a project
- **Size** (measure up the task in hand)
- **Weigh up** (judge the best means to ends)
- **Order** (prioritise and delegate tasks)

During a project
- **Test** (check progress against objectives, and time limit)
- **Ahead** (predict if the project will be completed by the deadline)
- **Vary** (make any changes needed to achieve this goal)

After a project
- **Back** (reflect on what was achieved)
- **Question** (ask if you would do anything differently)
- **Headline** (summarise what you have learnt for next time)

***

Before a school trip
- **Connect** (link the destination with prior learning)
- **Picture** (visualise yourself being there)
- **Question** (wonder what might be found and found out)

On a trip
- **Listen** (notice and name special features of the destination)
- **Zoom** (think about some features or objects in particular)
- **Infer** (deduce or guess what lies behind the features or objects)

After a trip
- **Back** (recall highlights)
- **Respond** (answer questions about what you learnt)
- **Headline** (summarise what you learnt)

***

Planning Essays
- **Divide** (list what could go into the essay)
- **Group** (sort the ideas by theme/perspective)
- **Order** (arrange key points into a list of flowing paragraphs)

Writing an essay paragraph
- **Formulate** (suggest an idea or point)
- **Explain** (clarify how this relates to the question)
- **eXemplify** (give examples to support your point)

Writing an essay conclusion
- **Weigh up** (decide upon your side of the argument)
- **Maintain** (assert your point of view)
- **Justify** (give reasons for your decision)

***

Revision
- **Back** (recall what you have learnt)
- **Divide** (separate key terms)
- **Explain** (give their meanings or definitions)

Text comprehension
- **Keyword** (highlight the key words in the question)
- **Infer** (draw a conclusion from the text)
- **Respond** (answer the question)

Debating
- **Formulate** (suggest an idea for your side)
- **Justify** (argue for this idea)
- **Respond** (answer the opposition's ideas)

USING THINKING MOVES IN SCHOOL AND LIFE

Eighteen of the moves are particularly well suited for P4C enquiries. A teacher or facilitator who knows the moves well will see more clearly when there is a need for someone to **Respond** to a question or to **Justify** a claim. She or he might pick the best moment to ask everyone to **Zoom out** or perhaps to **Zoom in** on a particular idea.

We recommend that such moves be explicitly taught to students for the purposes of enquiry.

Eighteen is rather a lot to digest at once, of course, so we suggest splitting them into two groups of nine, starting with:

Back, Connect, Justify, Keyword, Listen, Negate, Question, Respond, Weigh up

It might be easier to think of them in a rough narrative order:

- **Listen** (pay attention to a stimulus – or to what people say)
- **Back** (recall what you have heard or seen)
- **Connect** (to other experiences or lessons you have had)
- **Question** (the meaning, truth and value of words or ideas)
- **Respond** (with answers or comments)
- **Negate** (disagree with a belief or position)
- **Justify** (argue for your position)
- **Keyword** (highlight important ideas)
- **Weigh up** (decide on your latest position)

The next nine, then, would be:

Divide, Explain, Formulate, Headline, Maintain, Test, eXemplify, Yield, Zoom

Here is a rough narrative order for these:

- **Formulate** (suggest a new way of thinking)
- **Test** (put what someone has said in doubt)
- **Maintain** (commit to a belief or position)
- **Explain** (say how you think things are)
- **Headline** (summarise what you think others are saying)
- **e** (give an example to clarify or support your position)
- **Divide** (separate, or distinguish between, ideas and positions)
- **Zoom** (out – i.e. survey what people have said)
- **Yield** (accept others' point of view)

Each of these 18 moves, with the bracketed explanations, is on an A5 sheet that can be downloaded from the support resources. We would recommend that facilitators distribute these so that enquirers during P4C can look for opportunities to 'make the move', or notice when the move is made by others. (The latter can also be done by observers in an outer circle or fishbowl arrangement, which would be good practice for metacognition.)

There are eight more moves not listed above. Most of them can also be used in enquiry, for developing deeper, more critical thinking, but some of them may be regarded as useful more widely, in routine teaching or in everyday life. So, here is the third set:

Ahead, Group, Infer, Order, Picture, Size, Use, Vary, Zoom in

These do not so easily form a narrative order, but here are suggestions as to how they could also be useful in the classroom:

- **Ahead** (predicting consequences of actions)
- **Group** (sorting or classifying)
- **Infer** (deducing conclusions or implications)
- **Order** (putting things in order of priority)
- **Picture** (visualising, or even putting yourself someone's shoes)
- **Size** (estimating the scale of a claim or of a problem)
- **Use** (trying out a proposal in class or perhaps a 'thought experiment')
- **Vary** (changing perspective or focus)
- **Zoom in** (focussing on a key word or proposition)

A final thought for this section: whilst this book is written primarily for teachers and use in classrooms, the moves are not a merely academic device. They include almost all the possible moves that a thinker could make in any circumstance. So, they are equally appropriate for everyday purposes, such as organising events or running businesses. The skill set needed by a chair of a committee is very similar to that of a teacher conducting a classroom enquiry.

MEMORISING THE MOVES

Educators who advocate more of a focus on the explicit teaching of thinking are often misrepresented as being against the teaching of 'knowledge' – as if there is no knowledge, anyway, about either thinking or teaching! (One only has to think of the vocabulary, such as **Infer** or **Justify**, that one needs to know in order to perform even basic moves of logic, to appreciate the strawness of that argument.)

We not only accept the need to teach knowledge as a basis for good thinking and judgement, but also accept rote learning can sometimes be a good thing. Indeed, we believe that learning the moves by heart would be of great value for both everyday and academic purposes. This is because having them ready to mind enables one both to employ them more skillfully oneself, but also to elicit them more systematically from others (a bit like de Bono's Thinking Hats, or his handy mnemonics, PMI, AGO, CAF, etc.)

We maintain, moreover, that young minds, and even older ones, can memorise the moves very quickly and thoroughly.

Apart from the fact that the alphabet provides an easy series of pegs on which to hang the moves, they also come in a number of pairings, which almost halve the job of memorising. Some pairs even have the convenience of being consecutive, as follows:

- **Ahead/Back** (in time)
- **Connect/Divide** (in space)
- **Explain/Formulate** (an idea)
- **Infer/Justify** (a conclusion)
- **Maintain/Negate** (a claim)
- **Question/Respond** (obviously?)
- **Size/Test** (a claim)
- **Use/Vary** (an idea)

Others pair quite well at a distance:

- **Group/Order** (items)
- **Headline/Keyword** (main ideas)
- **Listen/Picture** (words/worlds)
- **Weigh up/Yield** (considerations)
- **eXemplify/Zoom** (particular/general)

Discussion of the different ways in which these pairs connect (e.g. opposites, complements, varieties) can help students not only remember the moves but also understand and appreciate them better.

1. We recommend you give students a copy at once of the master sheet of moves (i.e. with their key partners) that can be found on p. 5. You can download an A4 sheet from the website.

2. Have a quick run through of the list, asking students to tick off every move they have heard of before, along with the synonyms they've heard of. Don't worry about explaining each move at this point.

3. If a move is not familiar to most students (the most likely are: **Formulate**, **Infer**, **Justify**, **Maintain**, **Negate**, **Size**, **Test**, **eXemplify**, **Yield** and **Zoom**), ask them to look at the synonyms and tick off one or both if they've heard of them. Take time to explain a move if the synonyms, too, are unfamiliar to some.

4. Go back to the start of the list and point out the pairings above. Spend time discussing them if it's helpful.

5. End this first session by giving each student a blank A–Z (download from the website). In pairs, they should fill in as many of the moves as they can (without looking at their master sheets). Then tell them they will be given another written quiz in pairs at the end of the week. Make the process fun rather than a chore. If suitable, you could offer prizes for the most successful pairs. Just be prepared with enough prizes for everyone to succeed!

Learning the moves is most effective if it is reinforced two or three times in the first few weeks – so move as quickly as you can from the written test to oral reciting of the A–Z, then perhaps try the Z–A. (Don't be shy of whole class reciting!) Refer to the moves as often as you can in lessons in between testing. They are intended for regular mention and mobilisation. Before long, you and your students will be so familiar with them that you might appoint a couple of 'Moves Monitors' each lesson, whose job it is to identify the use and user of several moves per lesson.

A final tip: it would be desirable for your students to 'own' the moves as quickly as they can. A simple way of doing this would be to allocate a different move each lesson to each student. S/he could then monitor the use of that particular move. Ideally, s/he would note down the name of the user as well as the context of its use. You won't have time to have all the moves made public at the end, but you could check off one or two each time, especially those less common or less easy to identify. You could give bonuses to students who report using 'their' move in other lessons or in their everyday lives. Time invested in such reporting early on will pay dividends in students' increasing competence in implementing the moves in future.

CONNECTIONS WITH OTHER THINKING SCHEMES

Beginning 20 years ago, Roger became more and more involved in the Thinking Skills movement – and especially Philosophy for Children (P4C). Professor Matthew Lipman, the author of P4C, remains one of the great contributors to the field, not least through Thinking in Education, and his autobiography, A Life Teaching Thinking.

Roger became increasingly concerned, though, about the vagueness and controversies surrounding Thinking Skills. He became concerned, also, that he was promoting P4C as a way of developing thinking in schools without a clear sense – indeed, list – of the different sorts of thinking he was trying to promote.

To be fair, he had elaborated Lipman's framework of Critical, Creative and Caring Thinking into the widely used P4C framework (with Collaborative Thinking as the fourth 'leg'); and, like many a P4C practitioner, drew on Teaching for Better Thinking by Ann Margaret Sharp and Laurance Splitter, two of Lipman's leading associates.

There were many lists of thinking skills. Frameworks for Thinking, published in 2005 by a team led by David Moseley, reviewed no fewer than 42 such schemes. Yet none were what teachers needed them to be: easy to explain to students and easy for students to memorise. It was when Roger attended a workshop on Habits of Mind, led by Art Costa, nearly 10 years ago that he conceived of the possibility of constructing a memorable list of distinct acts of thinking.

It could be argued that the most famous scheme, Bloom's taxonomy – fulfilled these needs, having just six main categories that were fairly easy to grasp. But, quite apart from controversies about its apparently hierarchical structure, and its omission, on the face of it, of vital categories such as reasoning, it has been more of a teachers' than a students' scheme, as has the 19-category version published by Lorin Anderson and David Krathwohl in 2001.

What was needed was not so much a theoretical construct of human thinking but a matter-of-fact, methodical and memorable way of thinking about one's thinking, without resort to technical terms. That is how the A–Z was conceived and, as indicated in the previous section, it was constructed through regular reflection on thinking in practice – through metacognition, no less! From the start it used the language of moves rather than skills, so that it could analyse thinking more precisely – as steps to be taken, rather than complex or subtle strategies.

Finally, Roger mapped the moves methodically to the letters of the alphabet – employing the most natural mnemonic to assist in learning the moves.

TRAINING

While Thinking Moves A–Z is remarkably easy to access, it is worth investing in training in the use of the framework. This will ensure that you know how to establish it in the right way, and can get the most out of it for your students. Once you've done the training, you'll be ready to use it in class straightaway – and you'll also have a vision of how to develop it over the longer term.

We offer a one-day Thinking Moves A-Z training course that will:

• Familiarise you with Thinking Moves A–Z and show you different ways to introduce it to your students so that they can quickly memorise and own it;

• Show you how to enrich inquiry-based learning programmes, such as Philosophy for Children, by incorporating Thinking Moves;

• Show you how to build Thinking Moves into the main curriculum, or into specialist thinking skills, study skills and life skills courses;

• Give you practical guidance on how to embed Thinking Moves A–Z in your school's overall approach to teaching and learning.

The format of the training is flexible: it can be a single full day, two-half days or three twilight sessions. We offer it on a whole-school basis for teams of up to 25 teachers, or for individual teachers on open courses. We can provide bespoke courses for applications outside mainstream school, such as parent groups, vocational or professional training and life-skills organisations. All our trainers, including Roger, Tom and Jason, are accredited in Thinking Moves A–Z and inquiry-based learning - and we can offer our training worldwide.

As well as the training courses, we offer a growing range of supporting resources to help you implement Thinking Moves A – Z in your classroom or study group, including classroom posters, lesson plans and a survey-based evaluation tool to monitor teacher and student progress in adopting Thinking Moves and its impact on metacognition.

For details of our training courses and resources, please refer to our websites, or you can just search for "Thinking Moves A – Z training"

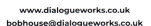

www.dialogueworks.co.uk
bobhouse@dialogueworks.co.uk

www.thephilosophyman.com
jason@thephilosophyman.com

ABOUT THE AUTHORS

Roger Sutcliffe studied Philosophy and Modern Languages at Oxford, and later took an Open University degree in Maths and Educational Management. He did voluntary work in India before a teaching career at both junior and secondary schools. He trained in 'Philosophy for Children' (P4C) with Matthew Lipman in New Jersey, and in Creative Thinking with Edward de Bono in Malta. He also qualified as a Rogerian (!) counsellor in UK.

Roger was a founder member of SAPERE, the UK charity for promoting P4C, and is a former Chair and President. He is a former President of ICPIC, in which over 60 countries practising philosophy with children are represented. He has trained thousands of teachers, including a stint as an Associate Lecturer on the MA course in Teaching Philosophy at Heythrop.

He is a consultant for Thinking Matters and also a director of **P4C.com**, the online resource and collaboration service for P4C worldwide and of DialogueWorks (**www.dialogueworks.co.uk**) which trains teachers in the UK and abroad. He co-authored 'The Philosophy Club', 'Newswise' and 'The Pocketbook P4C'.

Jason Buckley is the founder of The Philosophy Man. He has practiced P4C with thousands of participants, from nursery age through to undergraduates and teachers. He is author of minibooks Pocket P4C, Thinkers' Games and Philosophy Circles (with Tom). Over 17,000 teachers around the world receive his free weekly bulletin of resources, which you can sign up for at **www.thephilosophyman.com**

He is also Director of Studies at GIFT, the UK's leading provider of enrichment courses for the most able children, and founder of Outspark, which runs DofE Expeditions. He lives on a narrowboat and enjoys caving and musical comedy improv.

Tom Bigglestone is Philosopher-at-Large at The Philosophy Man. He has taught at primary and secondary level in both state and independent schools, including as Head of Humanities. Over the past ten years he's got students thinking in Religious Studies, English, History and Geography, as well as on the sports field.

He often writes despatches from the classroom for the The Philosophy Man bulletin. Tom is also particularly interested in how progress can be assessed in philosophy - the subject of his research for the Walter Hines-Page Scholarship in 2014.